Original title:
A Symphony of Snowfall

Copyright © 2024 Creative Arts Management OÜ
All rights reserved.

Author: Evelyn Hartman
ISBN HARDBACK: 978-9916-94-610-7
ISBN PAPERBACK: 978-9916-94-611-4

Whispers of Winter's Embrace

Snowflakes tumble down with flair,
Dancing hats upon the air.
Snowmen giggle, round and bright,
Lost their noses in the night.

Sleds go zooming, laughter flies,
Chasing tales beneath the skies.
A penguin slides, oh what a sight,
Wearing shades, he's feeling right.

Frosted Melodies of the Night

Icicles twinkle like the stars,
While hot cocoa warms our hearts.
Mittens slip, and snowballs fly,
Lands a laugh, oh me, oh my!

Chickens waddling, dressed in white,
They think it's time to take a flight.
Snowflakes whisper, 'Join the fun!'
As we hop around, all in one.

Dances of the Dancing Flakes

Flakes in pirouettes and spins,
Twirling hats and silly grins.
A fuzzy dog leaps with delight,
Wiggles in pure snowy white.

Children roll and giggle loud,
Making angels, so quite proud.
The frosty air, a laugh parade,
Each step, a dance, each turn, a trade.

The Language of Crystal Dreams

Whispers float on chilly air,
Tickled toes and frosty hair.
Grannies laugh in knitted gear,
Sipping tea, they have no fear.

A snowball fight, but wait... oh dear!
A surprise hit brings out a cheer.
In winter's clutch, we play and glide,
In this wonder, we all reside.

Choreography of the Cold

Flakes waltz down, all in a line,
A chilly parade, oh so divine!
Snowmen prance, with carrot noses,
They dance in circles, striking poses.

Ice on the rooftops, a slippery show,
Watch out below! Here comes a rogue snow!
Neighbors chuckle, on shovels they sit,
As snowballs fly, and laughter will split.

A Dance of Crystal Feathers

Feathers falling, soft and light,
Silly snowflakes flirt with the night.
They tickle noses, a freeze-frame cheer,
And catch on tongues, oh what a year!

Snowball fights, a frosty delight,
Giggles erupt, oh what a sight!
Slips and trips in this winter glee,
As snowflakes whisper, 'Catch me if you can!', with glee.

Snowy Whispers of the Heart

In winter's grip, we share a laugh,
With every snowman, a silly staff.
Toboggans zoom down hills like a dream,
While hot cocoa waits, steaming like a team.

Snowflakes giggle as they form a dance,
Frosty couples twist in a snowy romance.
Whispers of flakes echo in the air,
We stumble and trip, without a care.

Tumbling White Symphonies

Here comes a tumble, oh what a sight,
A snowball brigade, all ready to fight!
Laughs and giggles abound all around,
As children of winter jump from the ground.

Snowdrifts are stages for impromptu plays,
Where squirrels and snowmen hold their displays.
Flapping mittens, scarves that collide,
In this chilly wonderland, we take pride!

Luminous White Reverie

White flakes tumble down, oh so spry,
They tickle my nose as they pass by.
Snowmen dance under the moon's gaze,
With carrot noses and quirky ways.

Sledding down hills with a woosh and a cheer,
I scream with delight, no hint of fear.
But then I crash into a big snowdrift,
And all my laughter turns into a gift.

The Artistry of Ice

Icicles dangling from rooftops so grand,
Like nature's chandeliers, all carefully planned.
But one sharp drop lands right on my hat,
Oh, how I dance like a clumsy cat!

Snowflakes swirl in a waltz of their own,
Whispering secrets in a high-pitched tone.
If only they'd stop with their cunning tricks,
I'd catch them mid-air, not just in snow drifts!

Soft Notes in a Snowy Veil

Soft powder blankets the world with delight,
Kids giggling loud on this frosty night.
They build forts like experts, so bold,
But it's me who gets pelted with snowballs of cold!

In snowball fights, I'm a warrior true,
Yet every round ends with a face full of goo.
I launch my best shot with all of my might,
But land in a snowbank, oh what a sight!

Glistening Silence

Silence reigns where the snowflakes fell,
But wait—what's that? A cat's ringing bell!
As they prance and leap in their winter play,
I join their chaos, come what may!

A snowdog appears, with a tail made of fluff,
He rolls in the snow, can't get enough!
Laughter erupts, our hearts full of glee,
In this world of white—pure jubilee!

Starlit Frost

Snowflakes dance, a giggly spree,
Frosty noses, oh, what a sight!
Sleds on hills, we tumble free,
Laughter echoes in the night.

Chasing flurries, slipping quick,
Snowman dreams in hats adorned,
Belly flops and snowball flicks,
Winter's games, forever scorned!

Hot cocoa's warmth, we take a sip,
Marshmallows float like fluffy dreams,
Snowball fights become the trip,
In chilly whims, we're bursting seams!

As snowflakes twirl, we spin around,
Falling hearty, with joy we shout,
The wintry world, enchantingly bound,
In frosty fun, there's never doubt!

Serendipity of the Cold

Here comes winter, with a grin,
Slippery streets, watch out for slips!
Snowmen sigh, 'Let us begin!'
With carrot noses and funny quips.

Out come mittens, mismatched flair,
Taking bets on who will fall.
It's a snowball showdown, we all share,
With giggles and shrieks, we have a ball!

Snowflakes whisper secrets, bright,
Falling softly on our heads.
We juggle snowballs left and right,
Until someone trips and dreads!

A flurry of fun, that's what we seek,
With every tumble, hearts take flight.
In winter's chill, we find our peak,
Laughing through the starry night!

Melting Away in Silence

Icicles hang like frozen teeth,
Beware the drip, it may surprise!
Under the snow, a hidden wreathed,
A treasure hunt beneath the skies.

Woolly hats, they won't stay put,
As we chase the fluff, giggling loud.
Frosty fingers, toes in soot,
Winter mischief, we're so proud!

The cozy fire, it starts to pop,
With stories told of snowy fails.
As snowflakes fall, we just can't stop,
Catching dreams in chilly gales.

With every laugh, the hours fly,
But soon we'll know the warmth will call.
As seasons shift and snow bids bye,
We'll recall this winter's crazy ball!

Dance of the Frozen Breeze

Flakes twirl and swirl with glee,
Making snowmen, sip hot tea.
Laughter born on icy air,
Ice skates sliding without a care.

Penguins march in silly lines,
Chasing snowflakes, dodging pines.
Mittens find their way to friends,
Snowball fights that never end.

Sleds go zipping, laugh till bright,
Winter wonderland feels just right.
But who slipped on that frozen patch?
A comedy show, some winter match!

Giggling kids joyfully shout,
Winter's here, let there be no doubt.
Sliding down the hills they race,
In this cold, they find their space.

Chilling Overture

To the sound of chilly sneeze,
Snowmen wobble in the breeze.
Winter hats don't match their coats,
Fluffy muffs and soggy boots.

A snowflake lands atop my nose,
And now my hot cocoa froze.
Mittens held up in the air,
A dance-off takes place without a care.

Snowball ammo piled up high,
Eager hands count 'one, two, fly!'
Unexpected splatters with surprise,
Friendship warms where laughter lies.

Chilly winds sing their sweet tune,
While neighbors frolic 'neath the moon.
Winter's fun in all the mess,
Who'd have thought it could impress?

Serene Echoes of Winter

In the quiet night, whoops and slips,
From snowy paths, we laugh and trip.
A cozy fire crackles bright,
While outside, we bring the light.

Snowshoes squeak as we all roam,
Each flake transforms into a poem.
Frolicking through flakes like raccoons,
Creating chaos beneath full moons.

Hot apple cider warms the soul,
As we plan our evening stroll.
Catch the snow on our tongues with glee,
Just watch your step, it's slippery!

Frosty mustaches, giggles fly,
Underneath the powdery sky.
Winter's charm plays tricks so sly,
With each tumble, we learn to fly!

The Whispering Blizzard

Whirling winds toss hats away,
Flying through snow, we choose to play.
It's a blizzard, but we don't care,
Snowmen sing, a frosty affair.

Socks that vanish, lose their pairs,
Skates go sliding, without any cares.
As the snow drifts rise and sway,
Laughter echoes, come what may.

Frozen fingers, we wiggle toes,
Chasing shadows, where nobody knows.
In this white wonder, we all collide,
Each frosty giggle, an icy ride.

A snowball flew, it took its choice,
A direct hit turned me to noise.
In the winter's chill, we find a thrill,
With every tumble, laughter's will.

Chords of Ice and Falling Light

Snowflakes jiggle, dance in air,
Twirling softly without a care.
Neighbors slip and slide with glee,
As winter plays its own marquee.

Frozen cheeks and noses bright,
A snowball fight brings sheer delight.
Everyone's laughter fills the street,
While frosty toes just can't take heat.

The trees wear blankets, pure and white,
While snowmen sport a hat for height.
In this concert, all partake,
With every slip, another break!

So grab your boots and join the fun,
With snowflakes falling one by one.
This chilly play, a joyful spree,
In frozen lands, we're all carefree.

Snowbound Serenade at Dusk

Whispers of snow in twilight's glow,
Frosty bites that make you go 'whoa!'
Children giggle as they slip,
Oh, what a jolly, icy trip!

Snowmen sporting crooked grins,
Waving at the passing winds.
Their carrot noses slightly askew,
Sending warm wishes, just for you.

Sleds zoom down the hilly slope,
A chilly rush, but full of hope.
In this chill, we'll dance and play,
Forget the cold, let laughter stay!

Hot cocoa waits, we'll dry our toes,
As winter smiles and gently glows.
This playful time beneath the stars,
Is a joy we'll carry near and far.

The Lullaby of Winter's Spirit

The flakes are singing as they fall,
A merry tune, a frosty call.
The dog is chasing, what a sight,
As shadows blend in pale moonlight.

Outside the door, the world's aglow,
With snowmen in rows, all in a row.
Their eyes of coal, so sly and keen,
Plotting mischief like a scene!

A blizzard's whisper brings cheer and fun,
As icicles hang like tales undone.
We huddle close, wrapped tight with glee,
In this melody of winter spree.

Snowballs fly in every direction,
Creating such a wild collection.
Yet in the chaos, joy stays true,
With hearts as warm as our favorite stew.

Crescendo of the Cold

In the stillness, snowflakes swirl,
An icy dance, a frosty whirl.
Giggles echo through the air,
As we build snow forts with great flair.

Frosty beards on kids abound,
With hats that tip and socks unbound.
Laughter rings out, a joyous sound,
In this frozen landscape, we are found.

Belly flops on sleds, what a thrill,
Each crash brings joy, a winter's chill.
With sliding snowmen close at hand,
Raucous fun is truly grand!

Yet once we tire from our play,
With noses rosy, heads sway.
We sip our cocoa, hands in mitts,
This winter symphony never quits.

Kaleidoscope of Cold

Flakes like feathers swirl and glide,
The dogs are hunting for a ride.
Snowmen wobble, buttons loose,
They tip and fall, what a funny moose!

Sleds are racing down the hill,
With kids in hot pursuit for thrill.
But whoops! A tumble, down they go,
Rolling 'round in cotton snow.

Snowball fights ignite the field,
Chucking balls, our arms must yield.
Laughter echoes, what a sight,
As snowballs fly with pure delight!

Beneath the stars, we stomp our feet,
And shuffle home, it's quite a feat.
So bundled up, we skip and hop,
Not wanting this cold fun to stop!

Winter's Embrace

Snowflakes landing on my nose,
Makes me laugh, like a ticklish pose.
Why did the tree wear a white cap?
Because it wanted a stylish wrap!

The frostbite bites with playful tease,
As we sip cocoa, oh so pleased.
Hot chocolate spills down my chin,
A winter treat, I'm in for a win!

Sliding down on icy tracks,
With laughter bursting from our backs.
Oops! I fell — but what a view!
All snowy and silly, just like you!

As icicles hang like silly toys,
We gather 'round, a group of boys.
And girls who giggle, cheeks aglow,
In winter's game, we steal the show!

Frosted Canvas of Peace

The world's a canvas, painted white,
With socked-toes dancing in the night.
Snowflakes fall like churros sweet,
But landing on my head, they cheat!

I tried to catch one on my tongue,
Instead, I found a frozen lung.
My breath comes out as puffs of steam,
Like winter's joke, or a funny dream!

In the park, a dog does race,
With snow and joy all over the place.
He jumps so high, oh what a show,
While I just stand and watch, aglow!

Snowy hats begin to fall,
As laughter echoes, one and all.
A frosted peace, a world so bright,
With jolly hearts that fill the night!

Celestial Drift

Stars above in softest glow,
While flakes descend, oh what a show!
One lands right on my icy hair,
And declares, "This winter's beyond compare!"

Dancing shadows, twinkling light,
Don't trip on snow, oh what a fright!
Skate and slip with flair and grace,
Oh dear, here comes a frosty face!

The world's a snow bowl, swirling fun,
With frosted giggles, 'til day is done.
When winter whispers in the night,
We hoot and howl with sheer delight!

So raise your cup of cocoa high,
Let's toast to flakes that flutter by.
In this cold breeze, our hearts take lift,
As we embrace the winter's gift!

Haunting Hues of Winter

Snowflakes dance in twisted pirouettes,
A frosty ballet, no one regrets.
Snowmen conspire with cheeky grins,
As we tumble in laughter, let the fun begin!

Icicles hang like fangs from the eaves,
Glistening gems that trick and tease.
But watch where you step, oh dear, oh no!
Your dignity's gone, like fresh fallen snow!

Winter whispers jokes, quite sly and shrewd,
As we bundle up, feeling slightly crude.
Laughter erupts with every snowball thrown,
With each playful chuckle, the chill feels like home.

When winter's breath howls and exclaims,
It's just mischief wrapped in frosty games.
So embrace the laugh and all the delight,
In this winter wonderland, everything's light!

Snow-Kissed Dreams

Each flake's a letter from Neptune's jest,
Or maybe it's Santa, simply undressed.
We sled down hills in ridiculous styles,
Making memories wrapped up in smiles.

The rooftops wear white like a bride at the ball,
But oh, how they wobble, let's hope they don't fall!
With snowball fights so sillily planned,
We play tag with frost, well-coordinated and grand.

Hot cocoa spills, with marshmallows afloat,
A sweet little party, oh what a gloat!
But watch for the pets, they've got quite the spree,
Leaving paw prints everywhere, just like graffiti!

As icicles melt, they drop like big tears,
A watery descent, fueled by our cheers.
So let the snow lay thick, let the laughter fly,
In this wintry embrace, let's reach for the sky!

A Silvery Soliloquy

In the silence, snowflakes whisper and jest,
Painting the world in a frosty fest.
Snowmobiles zoom, with drivers so bold,
Each crash and stumble, a story retold.

The snow's like frosting on a big, goofy cake,
While risqué snow angels, we curiously make.
A slippery slope becomes our fun ride,
With giggles and spills, it's a wild winter tide!

Frostbitten fingers count down to spring,
Yet here we are, making snowmen sing!
Snow forts are built with all of our might,
While snowballs soar in a frosty fight.

And when the sun shines, the warmth shines through,
We're left with our memories, a snow-covered skew.
So here's to the mishaps, the fun, and the cheer,
In this winter revelry, we've nothing to fear!

Frozen Phrases in the Chill

A frosty wind comes with quirky one-liners,
While snowflakes chat like gossiping timers.
We bundle up tight, like burritos of yarn,
And even the pugs wear scarves like a charm!

Snowball ballet in front of the pub,
There's a snow queen here, making a hubbub.
With every sleek glide, we clutch our warm mugs,
As hot drinks spill and unleash hearty shrugs!

When frost becomes art in a breathless display,
And ice-covered branches turn bright green to gray,
We laugh at our tumbling, our outings so grand,
In a world full of sparkles, life's quite unplanned!

So celebrate snow as it falls from the sky,
With chuckles and joy, let the frosty winds fly.
Embrace the absurd, with a frosty delight,
In this whimsical winter, let's frolic through the night!

The Quietude of Winter

The flakes are falling, quite the show,
A snowman's hat is way too low.
With carrot noses, they look absurd,
As frosty giggles can be heard.

Sleds zipping down the hill, oh dear!
A flying mitten, then a cheer!
Hot cocoa spills with every fall,
Winter's giggles are the call.

Chasing snowballs, taking aim,
I dodged one, but where's my fame?
Laughter echoes, like a song,
In the winter, we belong.

So here we dance, with silly glee,
Creating chaos, wild and free.
The quietude brings joy to play,
As winter whispers, "Hip hooray!"

Frosty Fables

Once upon a mountain grand,
A snowman tried to take a stand.
He wobbled on a stickly leg,
And danced with glee, quite like an egg.

A penguin sneezed, and oh what fun!
He slipped and landed on the run.
The snowflakes giggled in delight,
As frosty tales danced through the night.

The reindeer wore a funky hat,
They chuckled hard, a laugh, not flat.
With snowballs flying everywhere,
Each frosty fable fills the air.

So let us raise a glass up high,
To snowy tales that make us sigh,
In this winter wonderland bright,
We craft our laughs in pure delight.

An Ode to the Chill

Ode to the chill and freezing air,
Where warmth is rare and shivers flair.
The icicles hang with icy grace,
While noses freeze in this frosty place.

Snowflakes drifting with little care,
Land in your hair, oh what a scare!
A snowball fight, oh what a mess,
With laughter shared, we all confess.

In mittens thick, we waddle round,
Trying hard not to hit the ground.
Each tumble turns to fits of glee,
Oh winter, you're so fun, you see?

Let's roast some marshmallows by the fire,
Tell silly stories that we conspire.
In the chill, we find our thrill,
Who knew that winter could fit the bill?

Snowfall's Subtle Sonnet

With gentle grace, the snowflakes play,
They tumble down in a merry sway.
A dog runs by, all white and furry,
Chasing ghosts, in a delightful hurry.

While kids make angels on the ground,
The laughter rings; it's all around.
A squirrel slips, but look at that!
He shakes it off and chases a hat!

A snow globe spins with every turn,
Lights twinkle bright, where hearts can burn.
We dance through streets all covered white,
Winter's humor, pure delight!

Let cocoa steam and laughter soar,
There's something magical, never a bore.
In this realm of white, so neat and fine,
We find our joy, like sparkling wine.

Frost-Kissed Reverberations

Snowballs bounce, a winter cheer,
Chasing laughter, no need to fear.
Fingers numb, but spirits soar,
In this chill, we find much more.

Snowmen grin with carrot noses,
While squirrels plot in fluffy poses.
A slip, a slide, and down we go,
Who knew cold could steal the show?

Hot cocoa's warmth, a sip divine,
With marshmallows floating in line.
We toast to winter's clumsy grace,
In frosty fun, we find our place.

So let it snow, let blizzards freeze,
We'll dance and play with utmost ease.
In every flake that twirls and spins,
This frosty frolic, laughter wins.

Ethereal Blanket

A fluffy quilt on rooftops lies,
Just watch the cats with sleepy eyes.
They leap and pounce, oh what a sight,
In swirling fluff, a soft delight.

Snowflakes whisper, like tiny spies,
Falling gently from blue-grey skies.
The world transforms, a wondrous play,
Where socks and mittens lead the way.

Children bundle, out they dash,
Tobogganing in a snowy splash.
Giggling echoes fill the air,
Snowball fights without a care.

As night descends, our cheeks aglow,
We gather 'round for tales of snow.
With every giggle, frost takes flight,
In this winter magic, pure delight.

The Quiet Composition of Snow

A flake descends, it spins and twirls,
Making quiet dancers of all the girls.
They leap with grace, arms spread wide,
In this gentle flurry, joy can't hide.

Some say the flakes are tiny wishers,
Creating chaos with chilly swishers.
A scuffle here, a tumble there,
With frosty giggles filling the air.

The trees wear coats, so bright and white,
As snowmen plan their silly fight.
One's lost a hat, another's rolled wrong,
Yet all around, we dance along.

Under this blanket of frozen cheer,
We share our stories, loud and clear.
Each flake a note in winter's song,
In mischief's embrace, we all belong.

Sinfonia d'Inverno

The winter stage in white arrayed,
With cheeky critters, the mischief played.
A snowball's path, a hurried dodge,
Here comes the snow; it's time for charge!

Icicle chandeliers shimmering bright,
Offering laughter in the soft night.
With frozen noses and chilly toes,
The warmth of friendship brightly glows.

Snowflakes challenge each dancer's pose,
As we glide lands of cold repose.
A tumble, a roll, we laugh and cheer,
In winter's symphony, joy is near.

So let's embrace this frosty air,
With giggles and fun, without a care.
As snowflakes swirl and play their tune,
In winter's grip, we dance 'til noon.

Quiet Interludes in Nature's Choir

Snowflakes tumble, doing flips,
Building castles with their tips.
Squirrels with acorns, wearing frowns,
Are busy hiding—'cause winter's clowns.

The trees are dressed in gowns of white,
While penguins pull their hats in tight.
Chickadees giggle on frozen wires,
As winter's chill inspires fun fires.

Frogs are leaping, thinking it's spring,
Only to find it's still a fling.
They slip and slide on icy ponds,
Making sounds like rubbery wands.

So gather 'round in nature's pause,
Join in laughter, it's the best cause.
Snowballs fly, aiming for no names,
In this frosty game where all are players!

Frostbound Fantasies Under Moonlight

Bunny hops in boots of fluff,
Chasing shadows, playing tough.
Under the stars, it's all a race,
Frolicking in this frozen space.

The moon giggles, a silver spoon,
Lighting up the dancing raccoons.
They twirl 'round cacti, unaware,
That snow is falling, everywhere!

Snowmen wear hats like lopsided bowls,
With carrot noses, frozen goals.
With each snowball, a wild cheer,
"Better than summer!" is shouted, hear!

In this wonderland, giggles rise,
As penguins skate under starry skies.
Frosted dreams, quite a delight,
In this chilly, whimsical night!

Whispers of Winter's Dance

In the woods, a soft whisper calls,
A dancing snowflake gently falls.
The trees are swaying, caught in bliss,
Under this winter's frosty kiss.

Rabbits tumble, all paws in air,
As if they've joined a ballet fair.
The icicles drip like tiny tunes,
Singing songs under laughing moons.

Snowball fights in a frosty embrace,
Elves are giggling, off they race.
As penguins waddle, a sight to see,
Making jokes in snowsuit glee!

In the hush of night, the fun goes on,
With every snowflake, the laughter's drawn.
A chilly serenade fills the air,
As winter's magic dances everywhere!

Frosted Melodies

Snowflakes swirl in a frosty breeze,
As froggies jump with silly ease.
Slinking past on slippery ground,
They slip and slide—they've all been found!

A snowman eyes a passing deer,
With a carrot nose, he gives a cheer.
"Join our party!" he croaks with glee,
As snowballs splat—oh, can't you see?

Bouncing snowflakes, a playful tune,
Chickens in boots planning a swoon.
Winter wonders, giggles abound,
In this cartoonish, frosty ground!

So dance with the frost, let merriment start,
As snow plays the tunes of wintery heart.
With laughter echoing through snowy halls,
Nature sings, and joy enthralls!

Echoes of Frozen Dreams

Flakes swirling like dancers in the night,
They twirl and they leap in a comical sight.
Snowmen with scarves, all crooked and round,
Wobble 'til they fall with a hilarious sound.

Children all bundled, boots three sizes too big,
Tripping on laces, looking like a pig.
Snowball fights start, with grins ear to ear,
But landing on dad, sparks laughter and cheer.

Chill in the air, but smiles don't fade,
Each whoosh on a sled feels like a parade.
Winter's mishaps? Oh, what a delight,
As cheeks turn all rosy from sheer silly bites.

In the hush of the night, the world feels so bright,
Laughter echoes softly, everything's light.
With snowflakes like confetti, it all feels so grand,
A brief winter chuckle, all drawn in the sand.

Snowbound Serenade

Pillow fights echo, laughter fills the room,
Pajamas all mismatched, chaos a plume.
Hot cocoa spills, marshmallows afloat,
Mom's favorite mug, it's lost the nice coat.

Snow drifts outside, a glittery mess,
Neighbors all slip with a comical "yes!"
Building a fortress, no room for defeat,
A snow-castle crowned with a miniature seat.

The cat on the window, eyes wide, in awe,
Paws flailing quickly, stuck in the paw.
You'd think a snowbird was painted on glass,
But it's just a clumsy critter that's failed to pass.

Sledding down hills takes us right to the moon,
But landing in bushes? Well, that's just our tune.
Each tumble and fumble, we'll cherish till spring,
These moments of laughter, let their joy take wing.

Flurries of Imagination

In the garden of winter, where nonsense abounds,
Footprints of penguins make silly sounds.
Snowflakes like feathers fall soft and slow,
Creating a canvas, where mischief can flow.

A hat made of twigs, and a carrot for show,
Who knew a snowman could look like a crow?
The dog's playful leaps, his tail in the air,
He snatches a flake from his own furry lair.

Funny snow angels, all chaos and cheer,
Spread out on the ground, as giggles draw near.
Snowballs like cannonballs, aimed at the tree,
A hit from cousin Billy? Now that's pure glee.

Even the icicles seem to laugh and grin,
Their pointy formations like teeth from within.
In this world of white, let the fun count the miles,
As every cold gust brings forth our best smiles.

Hushed Tones of the Frost

With flakes softly falling, the world gets a fluff,
The quiet is sneaky, yet never too tough.
Whispers of snowflakes, they giggle and squeak,
Painting our towns with dreams, so unique.

Around every corner, a snowdrift awaits,
Lost rubber boots and miscalculated skates.
Mom's frown at the blanket that covers the yard,
Kids' laughter erupts, as snowballs get hard.

Even the squirrels wear a coat of white fury,
Chasing each other without any hurry.
They tumble and roll, as we all freeze and stare,
Winter's antics, we can't help but share.

In the glow of the streetlights, the magic unveils,
Snowmen tell stories of absurd little tales.
While frost paints the windows with whims of delight,
This chilly adventure wraps us through the night.

Crystal Lullabies

Flakes of white dance like clowns,
They tumble down in soft gowns.
Snowmen giggle with carrot noses,
While snowball fights turn to poses.

Sleds are flying, laughter rings,
Chased by snowballs, oh the flings!
A dog in boots, such silly sight,
Dashing off, oh what a fright!

Kids roll snowballs, big and round,
'Oh no!' they yell, 'Look what we've found!'
A snow angel with a crooked wing,
Flapping flurries—oh, what a fling!

Hot cocoa warms the chilly hands,
While marshmallows slide in snow lands.
"Is that a prince?" one giggles low,
"Or just my brother dressed in snow?"

Chilling Harmonies

Snowflakes fall in a wild dance,
Swirling 'round like they're in a trance.
Twirling children lose their hats,
Chasing snowmen, the cheeky brats!

One sneaky flake nests on a cat,
Who's confused about this chilly spat.
Cats can't leap in such big boots,
But they still glare while fluffing snoots!

With every toss, snowballs fly high,
Landing smack on brother's eye!
Giggles turn to playful shouts,
As snowflakes kiss, and winter pouts.

Sleds crash into soft, snowy hills,
With squeals of laughter, oh what thrills!
While parents sip on drinks quite hot,
Wondering how to get out of the spot!

Silence in the Snowflakes

In quiet ways the white stuff glows,
As it covers all the things it knows.
A squirrel sneezes and then it slips,
Down the hill with majestic flips!

In the stillness, a sound of clatter,
A toddler tumbles—oh, what a splatter!
Giggling loudly, he tries to rise,
With snowflakes stuck like little flies!

Snow angels form in every yard,
Making shapes and playing hard.
The dog just digs and rolls around,
While winter's magic knows no bound.

Carrot noses, buttons of coal,
Are used to make that jolly stroll.
Snowmen watch as kids collide,
In that fluffy chaos, side by side.

Winter's Gentle Caress

The sky wears white, a snowy cape,
While frosty air takes on a shape.
Giggling kids build towers tall,
Then sink down with a snowy fall!

Snowflakes giggle, they swirl and tease,
Landing on noses, they do as they please.
A kid slips on ice, what a surprise—
While everyone else rolls with the cries!

Sleds zoom past with a whoosh and a shout,
While old man Jenkins checks to see what it's about.
With frostbitten fingers, he shakes his head,
"Enough with the snow!" but it's all in good thread.

The cocoa's ready, marshmallows dance,
As friends gather 'round in snowy romance.
Joking and laughing till the daylight fades,
In the arms of winter, every fun cascade!

A Tapestry of White

Flakes twirl like dancers, full of glee,
Landed on hats, like a clumsy spree.
Snowballs form a secret pact,
Wage a war—oh, that's a fact!

Dogs chase tails in winter's flurry,
While kids zip past in a snowy hurry.
Snowmen sport hats too big to wear,
As snowflakes giggle in the chilly air.

Hot cocoa spills are quite the trend,
Sipping slowly, where do we send?
Marshmallows float like frosty dreams,
In this white chaos, nothing is as it seems.

When winter's curtain slips and falls,
Laughter echoes off the frosty walls.
With every slip and slide we take,
Joy finds us, in our snowflake wake.

Melodies Beneath the Snow

Snowflakes tap dance on the frozen ground,
Making tunes that are quirky, profound.
The frost hums softly a curious tune,
While squirrels are plotting a snack at noon.

Crisp leaves crinkle as kids romp around,
"Hurry!" they shout, "Let's make a mound!"
Laughter beams in the chilly air,
As snowballs land with a playful flair.

Gaggles of geese in formation swoop,
While snowflakes audition for a winter troupe.
Snowmen whisper secrets late at night,
Under the glow of soft, silver light.

Old stoves puff warmth from their hearth,
As tales of snow bring laughter and mirth.
With each little slip and every fall,
Winter's charm stitches joy into all.

Frost's Delicate Touch

Frosty paintbrush graces the trees,
Whispering secrets in the winter breeze.
Icicles dangle like nature's bling,
While dogs wear sweaters, oh what a thing!

Peering out, the world is a mess,
With snowflakes stuck in my hair, I confess.
Dreams of hot chocolate never get old,
Especially served in a mug that's bold.

Snow angels flaunt their practiced grace,
While laughter erupts in a chilly race.
Neighbors join in, building towers of snow,
With silly faces and hats all aglow.

When winter comes knocking, it brings delight,
Twinkling snowflakes dance through the night.
Together we giggle, with joy in sight,
In this frosty wonder, everything feels right.

Winter's Unseen Orchestra

Whispers in snow, a choir of hue,
Conducting the chill, it plays just for you.
Snowbanks see-saw as giggles ignite,
Each snowball launched brings comedic delight.

A cappella fun, the snowmen duet,
With carrot noses, none have a regret.
Frosted branches sway to the chill,
As we bundle up, enjoying the thrill.

Playful laughter spills with each slip and fall,
"Oh no, catch me!" as we scramble and call.
Winter's melody echoes, bright and clear,
Delighting our hearts, as we disappear.

Cookouts by fire with marshmallows aglow,
The sweetest of moments, in a frosty show.
As flakes blanket the world in white,
Life's little joys keep us cheery and bright.

Dreaming in White Hues

Flakes dance down with such great flair,
I catch one quick, it's in my hair.
A snowman grins with a carrot nose,
But melts away as the sunshine glows.

Snowballs flying with laughter loud,
Chasing friends, we feel so proud.
Slipping here and sliding there,
Winter's jokes give quite a scare!

My hot cocoa is now a drift,
Spilled it all, it's quite the gift.
Marshmallows floating, what a sight,
Sip too quick, and it spills outright!

Tonight we'll sled, let's race and steer,
With snowflakes tickling every ear.
When winter's done, I'll need a broom,
For all this joy will lead to gloom!

Tales Carried on the Winter Breeze

Whispers of snowflakes swim around,
They giggle softly, without a sound.
A squirrel skis on a frozen route,
While chatting up a cheeky trout.

With scarves that fly like colorful kites,
We twirl and spin on frosty nights.
Neighbors grumble, their shovels in hand,
But we're making igloos, oh so grand.

A snowball fight, who will prevail?
I aim for you, but I hit the mail!
With laughter echoing through the pines,
We plot our snow park kingdom designs.

As stars twinkle in the moonlit night,
Snowflakes giggle at our delight.
They might hold secrets, hints of their past,
But winter fun is what we hold fast!

A Ballet of the Falling Slush

Ballet dancers swirl in the sky,
Stumbling about, watch them fly!
They twirl and tumble, what a sight,
Landing on noses, pure delight.

Glistening coats, each one unique,
Furry hats causing sliding squeaks.
Trip over boots that seem too wide,
In this chilly dance, there's no guide.

Chasing snowflakes as they drift,
But lose my balance with a swift lift.
Down I tumble, no need to frown,
Start a snow angel on the ground!

There's laughter here, and friends abound,
Each snowy step brings joy profound.
As twilight paints the scene aglow,
We'll finish the dance with one last throw!

Glimmering Patterns in the Twilight

Twilight paints with sparkly white,
As snowflakes twirl in the fading light.
Each one's odd, like socks on hands,
They slip and slide, no winter plans!

We built a castle that fell apart,
Snow didn't like our sculptor's art.
The king of fluff, he waved goodbye,
As we laughed with our heads held high.

A raccoon breaks and then he slips,
He takes a dive, then flips and flops.
With every tumble, giggles grow,
Winter antics are the star of the show!

So here's to snow, it brings such glee,
With funny tales 'neath the old pine tree.
In icicle chandeliers, we will sway,
As night falls softly, let's laugh and play!

Glittering Signs of Winter

Flakes tumble down, a frosty dance,
Snowmen giggle, caught in a trance.
Penguins slide on their bellied zeal,
While squirrels chafe in an icy wheel.

Hot cocoa spills; the marshmallows float,
There's something odd about this white moat!
Jackets puffed like balloons in flight,
Dance in circles, what a silly sight!

The dog leaps high, just to flop,
In snowbanks deep, a fluffy plop.
The cat peeks out with a dismayed face,
Not sure if it's fun or a frozen race.

Snowballs fly, an unwritten rule,
Everyone's in it, the whole school.
Laughter rings like a chime on cue,
Who knew the chill could spark such a brew?

Celestial White Melodies

The skies release their frosty cheer,
Whirling flakes that appear quite queer.
Children dash with outstretched tongues,
Catching snow, humming winter songs.

Around the block, a snowball fight,
Who knew snow could bring such delight?
Faces red from the cold, they beam,
While snowflakes settle like a dream.

The trees wear coats of sparkling white,
A fashion show in the dim moonlight.
Critters scamper, looking for thrills,
Sliding down slopes, ignoring the chills.

The wind plays tunes, a real hoot,
Dancing branches in winter's boot.
With every gust, a laugh ensues,
Nature's joke, no one can refuse!

Frosted Fantasies

Icicles dangle like crooked teeth,
Nature's sculptures, with hidden wreaths.
A rabbit hops, thinks it's a clown,
With ears like floppy, snow-laden crowns.

Snowball dogs, all fluffy and bright,
Wreaking havoc, oh what a sight!
They chase their tails, then stuff their snouts,
In snowdrifts that amplify their shouts.

Giant footprints print the soft ground,
Where clumsy feet make joy abound.
Sliding mishaps cause a good crash,
Warm hearts emerge, with each silly splash.

In puddles that freeze, a laughter storm,
Winter's warmth in a quirky form.
As we stumble, slip, and frolic around,
The merriment of frost does astound!

Nature's Winter Waltz

Snowflakes twirl like dancers divine,
In a waltz of white, so cute and fine.
Snow-covered hills, our playground call,
With sleds and giggles, we'll have a ball.

Gloves and hats, all mismatched today,
Fashion disasters come out to play.
Our noses freeze, but we can't complain,
In this chilly realm, fun's never plain.

Snowmen grinning with carrot noses,
Dance with penguins and silly poses.
Laughter erupts from every flake,
A comical winter, for goodness' sake!

As twilight fades, we gather round,
Sharing tales of the goofiest sounds.
In this frosty wonder, can we lose?
Stirring memories, we all choose!

Snowflakes in Suspension

Tiny flurries dance and twirl,
Like little sprites in a winter whirl.
They tickle noses, freeze some toes,
And try to sneak in through each window.

Frosty giggles fill the air,
While mittens wobble, unaware.
Snowballs fly with gleeful might,
And scarves get tangled, what a sight!

Each snowflake holds a little joke,
A whisper of laughter in every poke.
As children tumble, cheeks aglow,
They wonder, where did all this snow go?

With every flake that falls and slips,
There's a chance for slips and icy trips.
But oh, the joy in winter's game,
Makes us giggle through the frame.

The Grace of Winter's Breath

Winter's breath is soft and sly,
Whispers that make grown-ups cry.
It sends their plans all in a tiff,
As they trip over a snow-laden drift!

The trees wear white like formal gear,
While squirrels shout, "Hey, winter's here!"
With paws on ice, they strut and slide,
Giving the snow a wild ride!

Snowmen laugh beneath their scarves,
That wobble and sway with winter's parves.
One carrot nose, two eyes that wink,
"Let's melt away! What do you think?"

And there we stand, hot cocoa in hand,
As flakes fall down like a comedy band.
So we'll dance and trip with all our might,
For winter's grace is sheer delight!

Silence Between the Flurries

Amidst the hush, a snowflake sneezes,
Causing chortles with winter breezes.
Each silent pause brings giggles tight,
As we watch the snow cascade in flight.

Hats fly off with a gusty glee,
Snowmen chuckle, "Look at me!"
A snowball fight—oh, what a mess!
As laughter echoes, we say, "Yes!"

The gentle flakes, with secret plans,
Plotting snowball ambushes with frozen hands.
We tiptoe lightly, hearts turned bright,
For each soft whisper begets pure delight.

When quiet reigns like a snowy crown,
We laugh away our winter frown.
Together we face this snowy affair,
Where silence brews mischief in the air!

Icy Harmonies

Icicles hang like slippery notes,
Creating tunes in chilly quotes.
Snowflakes dip and swirl with flair,
While polar bears dance without a care.

Frosty windows create silly doodles,
As cats chase shadows, pouncing poodles.
We hum along to winter's play,
As cooped-up critters find their way.

With every slip upon the ice,
Comes laughter that is oh so nice.
Snowball symphonies fill the air,
While children tango, unaware!

So grab your mittens, join the fun,
For winter's melodies have just begun.
In twinkling snow, we find our groove,
As chilly breezes make us move!

Shimmering Silence on Frozen Streets

In slippers I glide, with grace like a bee,
My dog's got the moves, he's fancy and free.
The snowflakes all dance, but why do they slip?
Watch out for that ice, I'm losing my grip!

Snowmen are built with noses askew,
They'd laugh if they could, what a funny crew!
A carrot for brains, they start to complain,
"Why'd you build us here? We're freezing our grain!"

The streetlights are twinkling, all covered in white,
I swear they just winked—what a magical sight!
But my nose is so chilly, it's red as a fruit,
Next time I'm wearing a spiffy old suit!

So here's to the days filled with laughter and cheer,
Though snowflakes may tickle, I'll always stay near.
With friends made of snow, life's a giggle, it's true,
Let's waddle and dance, like penguins do too!

Harmonies Beneath a Blanket of White

The world wears a coat, fluffy and thick,
I tripped on a mound, what a silly old trick!
Snowballs are flying, my aim is quite poor,
I duck from a flurry, then end up in more!

Kids making angels, all flailing and bright,
But one flaps away, it's a snow angel fight!
Giggles erupt as they tumble and roll,
Is winter a game that can steal all your soul?

The snowflakes all play hopscotch in the air,
While snowmen debate if they'll ever be rare.
"Do you hear that?" one says with a grin on his face,
It's just my old boots, they've decided to race!

So here we are laughing under skies of gray,
Transforming the chaos, in our funny way.
With snowmen and laughter, we'll make quite a stand,
Their jokes leave my sides sore—it's truly unplanned!

Celestial Waltz of the Snowflakes

Floating down gently, the flakes have a plan,
To soften my walk like a soft, puffy fan.
But soon they team up with some wind in the mix,
To toss me around like a bag full of tricks!

Sledding downhill turns into a grand chase,
I went for a ride and lost all my grace!
Who knew I could tumble, both me and my sleigh?
I'm honestly not sure that I want to stay!

The flakes start to chatter, as if they can talk,
They giggle and swirl in a wild, frosty flock.
"Watch out for that kid, he's got way too much speed!"
But here I am, laughing, I just want to lead!

So dance with the winter, let's twirl in delight,
With giggles and chaos that stretch into night.
This chilly parade is a hoot, can't you see?
Come join in the fun, and just frolic with me!

Echoes of Winter's Gentle Touch

Softly the white spreads like icing on cake,
I stepped in a puddle, instead of a flake!
Now wet socks in winter, it's really quite grim,
"Next time, dear foot, let's not be so dim!"

The squirrels are confused, they make goofy leaps,
Hiding their acorns in snow, not in heaps.
They chatter and scamper, so quick on their feet,
It's a comedy show on this cold, snowy street!

With snow on my nose, I join in the fun,
Making snow angels while the dog loves to run.
But when I get up, oh dear, what a sight,
It's an angel that's missing its head—what a fright!

So here's to the winter, where laughter is found,
In slips, trips, and giggles, all around we are bound.
Let's chuckle together, let's savor the bliss,
For joy in the snow is the sweetest of gifts!

The Stillness of Flurries in Flight

Tiny flakes dance like cats on the floor,
They twirl and they spin, asking for more.
The ground starts to giggle, the trees start to sway,
As snowmen complain, 'It's too chilly today!'

With snowballs for snacks, we launch them in glee,
They splat on the dog, oh what a sight to see!
A muffled laugh comes from an unsuspecting post,
As the world takes a snooze, but we're laughing the most.

Melodic Nuances of a Winter's Night

The sky plays a tune with each floppy white flake,
A symphony strange, like a cat with a shake.
Pine trees are swaying to a rhythm so grand,
While snowmen are whistling without a whole band.

With boots full of fluff and mittens on tight,
We skate on the sidewalk, it's a comical sight.
I tumble and roll, oh what a disgrace,
As I get off the ground, there's a smile on my face.

Enchanted Dreams Under Frosted Stars

Stars twinkle above in the chilly night air,
While frosted dreams slip without a care.
Snowflakes are piled high on the fence,
Each one with a secret, it's utterly intense!

A snow fort was built, my fortress of cheer,
I'm king of the winter, come join me, my dear!
But wait, here comes Ralph with a chuckle and dash,
He's aiming my way with a snowball of smash!

Collecting Snowflakes Like Secrets

I catch little snowflakes on my tongue with delight,
Each one has a story, a twinkle, a bite.
I giggle and wiggle, they swirl all around,
With each chilly kiss, my laughter is found.

While sledding down hills and dodging the trees,
We're flying with laughter, all care in the breeze.
Yet, here comes a tumble, a fall full of grace,
As I cradle my snowball like a doll in a space.

Echoes on a White Canvas

Look at the flakes, all spinning around,
They dance on the streets, without making a sound.
Chasing each other, they giggle and play,
Trying to cover my boots in a white display.

A snowman's grin, with a carrot for a nose,
He's making me laugh, who knows how he knows?
He's got a scarf and a top hat, looking so grand,
But I think he's plotting to make a snowband!

When snowballs soar through this chilly expanse,
I dodge and I weave, but I can't help but glance.
That kid over there, with his goggles and gear,
Looks like he's ready for a snow ninja career!

Oh, frozen cheeks and toasty hot cocoa,
Laughter erupts with each slippery glyphosate.
The world is a canvas, painted in white,
Let's laugh at the chaos, until it feels right!

Frosty Trails of Night

Under the moon, the snow softly glows,
Each step that I take, it crunches and flows.
With socks on my hands and a hat for a crown,
I waddle like penguin while walking through town.

Icicles dangle from rooftops with glee,
They look like frozen creatures just waiting to flee.
As I toss and I tumble in this wintery blight,
I swear I just heard a snowman ignite!

The sidewalks are slick, I slide with a grin,
Funny, it feels like I'm training to spin.
The neighbors all peek through their frosty glass frames,
Chuckling and pointing at my spontaneous games!

Bright lights spark joy in this frosty affair,
Snowflakes keep spinning through the chilly night air.
We laugh at the madness that comes with the chill,
For winter, it seems, has a comical thrill!

The Softness of Snowfall

Feathers from heaven, the sky's gentle gift,
Each flake on my nose gives my spirits a lift.
I stomp in the drifts, feeling like a big kid,
With snowmen in progress, all dreams that we hid.

A snowball brigade marches right up to the door,
But I'm armed with marshmallows, a fluffy encore!
With laughter and giggles, the battle begins,
Who knew that snow would be riddled with grins?

Oh, cozy and warm in my wardrobe so tight,
I ponder the wonders of this frosty sight.
The air is so crisp, it tickles my nose,
I am a snowflake detective; let's see how it goes!

Sledding down hills on a seat made of joy,
Just me and my friends, oh what fun to employ!
With a splash and a crash, we land with delight,
Creating this chaos feels so perfectly right!

White Soundscapes

In a world of white whispers, we stroll with the crew,
Snowflakes are falling, as if on cue.
We weave through the trees, like a holiday dream,
With laughter and antics, it's one splendid theme.

A snowball flies past; I duck and I laugh,
Imagining penguins out with their giraffe.
We build frozen towers, an icy ballet,
Oops! There goes the hat – is that one made of hay?

Snowflakes like candy dance down from the skies,
They settle on noses and cover our eyes.
Look at that snowman all dressed up so bright,
He's stealing my heart with his silly delight!

So here's to the fun and the chill in the air,
With punchlines and snowdrifts as fluffy as care.
Let's toast with our mugs, to this whimsically white,
And giggle like children beneath the moonlight!

Snowbound Impressions

Snowflakes flutter, wild and free,
Landing on my nose, oh, what glee!
I build a man, but he's so stout,
He tips and rolls - we laugh and shout!

Winter's chill, a frosty tease,
Hot cocoa waits, with marshmallows, please.
We sled down hills, a bumpy ride,
Like clumsy penguins, we slip and slide!

Boots are soaked, scarves all askew,
My dog leaps high, like he's brand new.
He steals my glove, with a cheeky bark,
Chasing his tail – quite the funny lark!

As night falls down, the moon's a glow,
Starlight dances on melted snow.
We dream of warmth, of sunny sights,
But first, another snowball fight!

Dance of the Crystal Veil

Flakes pirouette, in breezy flight,
Tickling faces, what a delight!
A frosty twirl, a chilly waltz,
My hat flies off – such snowball faults!

Winter's stage, where giggles resound,
We tumble softly, barely rebound.
Snowmen wink, with a twinkly eye,
I trip and fall – oh my, oh my!

Snow angels flap, but I make a mess,
Laying down sure won't impress!
I've got the grace of a sleepy bear,
Flapping my arms, without a care!

With rosy cheeks, we bounce and play,
Tasting snowflakes, sweet as a parfait.
As I dash forward, a slip and a shout,
Who knew a snowball brings such a clout?

Quiet Steps in the White

Softly we march, in fluffy white,
Wishing for mischief, it feels so right.
A crisp step forward, oh what a sight,
I trip on a branch, a comical fright!

Birds give a chirp, looking so slick,
While I'm clad in winter gear, thick as a brick.
They mock my style with a feathered cheer,
I chuckle back – what do they know here?

Frosty whispers float through the air,
I sneeze loudly, I hope none would stare.
Snow scatters everywhere, a soft poof,
As I look up, I lose my roof!

The world in white, a cozy dream,
But slipping and sliding is not what it seems!
Yet silly laughter warms the cold,
Each frosty patch, a joy to behold!

Frost's Gentle Ballad

Hush now, listen, the snow's singing low,
With a giggle here, and a giggle there, oh!
Carrot noses on snowmen stand,
They seem to grin, feel free to expand!

Little feet patter, with cheers and squeals,
Tumbling giggles in frosty seals.
Rabbits hop by, with fluffy coats,
While I try to catch them, I miss those folks!

Where are the snowballs? A launch is in sight,
I fling one wide, and it's quite a fright!
It's aimed at my pal, oh what a dodge,
He throws back faster, we're ready to lodge!

Under the stars, the curtains pull tight,
Snowflakes dance in the silver moonlight.
In frosty fun, we fondly stay,
Singing sweet carols 'til the break of day!

Milton Keynes UK
Ingram Content Group UK Ltd.
UKHW022341171124
451242UK00007B/75

HIS

TIES THAT BIND DUET

A. ZAVARELLI
NATASHA KNIGHT

Copyright © 2020 by A. Zavarelli and Natasha Knight

All rights reserved.

Cover Design by Coverluv

No part of this book may be reproduced in any form or by any electronic or mechanical means, including information storage and retrieval systems, without written permission from the author, except for the use of brief quotations in a book review.

This is a work of fiction. Names, characters, businesses, places, events and incidents are either the product of the author's imagination or used in a fictitious manner. Any resemblance to actual persons, living or dead, or actual events is purely coincidental.

NOTE FROM THE AUTHORS

HIS is the second and final book of the Ties that Bind Duet. You must read book 1, *MINE*, first in order to follow the story.

Mine is available in all stores now.